UNDRESSING UNDER THE NOON SUN

CHARITY HUTETE

Published by Akashic Books
©2019 Charity Hutete

ISBN: 978-1-61775-745-7

Printed in China
First printing

Akashic Books
Brooklyn, New York, USA
Ballydehob, Co. Cork, Ireland
Twitter: @AkashicBooks
Facebook: AkashicBooks
E-mail: info@akashicbooks.com
Website: www.akashicbooks.com

African Poetry Book Fund
Prairie Schooner
University of Nebraska
110 Andrews Hall
Lincoln, Nebraska 68588

TABLE OF CONTENTS

PREFACE
by Nick Makoha

The lens of Charity Hutete's book falls directly on her country of Zimbabwe. Her musings open us up to the sensibilities of the Shona people, through a language intentionally direct in its simplicity of diction, which belies a complexity of thought and feeling in a manner that brings to mind the work of Lucille Clifton.

Poetry, for Charity Hutete, who works for a Zimbabwe-based NGO to address the issues her country faces head-on, provides her with a platform on which she is able to voice her concerns to the wider world; not through the metrics of economics, demographics, reports, and strategic plans, but through the force of language, of feeling, of music, and of metaphor with depth, sophistication, and deep feeling.

Her poetry is plainspoken, clean-lined, and to the point. However, this does not diminish her wit, imagination, and passion. Politics and poetry can only be uttered with intention.

It is clear to me that Hutete is seeking to construct, with language—with words—what Audre Lorde called the "new world" when she said:

> Words had an energy and power and I came to respect that power early. Pronouns, nouns, and verbs were citizens of different countries, who really got together to make a new world.[1]

What the poet knows is that silence will not protect her. Hutete shows faith in language's ability to surpass common logic and makes full use of poetry's capacity to sustain a political charge and to share her wisdom. This has long been the tradition of the poet: to both observe and question our humanity.

Her work is driven by a willingness to speak with clarity and pain-

---

1. Karla M. Hammond, "Audre Lorde: Interview," *Denver Quarterly* 16, no. 1 (1981).

ful candor about the challenges facing her country and her people. Using efficient and precise symbolism, she offers parables that present the reader with a portrait of a nation and a region in which people suffer. In "Raking leaves," a poem of deep pessimism, she employs a Sisyphean-like allusion to describe the futility of effort in the face of a certain fatalism. The speaker finds herself raking leaves fallen from a barren tree, a tree that does not bear fruit and will not assuage the hunger of the labourer:

> There will be no pips
> between our teeth at day's end,
> just dried leaves, so we'll build
> all manner of castles with peat.

The Zimbabwe she describes is not the vaunted "breadbasket of Southern Africa." Instead, she presents a different, more alarming reality. In this and other poems, Hutete shows how the body suffers in this unyielding land whose former glory is reduced to peat. The vision is painfully affecting:

> We rake, amassing dried leaves.
> No sooner are they gathered than they
> are blown away by the slightest wind.
> So we'll rake in perpetuity
>
> until the rake depletes our strength
> and the spade burrows a mouth
> in the earth for the tree to devour
> our shrivelled remains.

And yet, we have been prepared for this kind of truth-telling from the first few lines of the collection. The poet has prepared us to introduce a peculiar alchemical process to our imagination—how to take despair and transform it into something extremely hopeful.

As the first poem in the chapbook, "An African Roadmap," suggests, this collection of poems constitutes a poetic cartography that seeks to chart the psychic, political, economical, and moral topography of the continent. In this poem, the black and white symbolism, the neatly drawn conceit, is blunt in its critique of the racial realities of Zimbabwean geopolitics:

> Everywhere,
> the black tar wide and long
> reaching even the land's horn
> is divided by very thinly spread
> white stains which run along its core
> determining who goes in which
> direction and who stops where.
>
> The tar enraged,
> chews itself from the edges.
> It may consume itself completely
> before it's free of the stain.

Even as Hutete speaks of the ruins of Zimbabwe's roads purging themselves, there are echoes of Nelson Mandela's essay "African Renaissance" and his blunt statement about the destruction of Carthage in Tunisia at the vengeful hands of the Roman Empire: "Only our African being," he wrote, "makes it possible for us to hear the piteous cries of the victims of the vengeance of the Roman Empire." But from this place of destruction and lament, he articulates a core principle of possibility similar to that which seems to rest at the center of Hutete's verse:

> And yet we can say this: that all human civilization rests on foundations such as the ruins of the African city of Carthage. These architectural remains like the pyramids of Egypt, the sculptures of the ancient kingdoms of Ghana and Mali and Benin, like the

temples of Ethiopia, the Zimbabwe ruins and the rock paintings of the Kgalagadi and Namib deserts—speak of Africa's contribution to the formation of the condition of civilization. [2]

In Hutete's defiant poem "Clouds Are Gathering," it is hard to miss this stern pragmatism in the face of disaster—a fulsome faith in the very redemption that Mandela speaks of. Here is Hutete writing in her most eloquent and direct manner:

> Clouds are gathering overhead.
> The wind's singing crescendos.
> Everyone's shutting their windows
> and swallows are waltzing the skies.
>
> All are bracing for the storm.
> I, too, should be running for cover
> but here I am lying face up
> in an open meadow, thirsty.
>
> I welcome the tempest's baptism,
> exorcist of stubborn fears.
> Countless trying droplets
> push against the mind's
>
> margins, deliberate breakers
> determined to devastate and
> reinstate in the same wash, a pond
> plied into a pulsing river.
>
> Surprising how strength becomes me.

2. "African Renaissance," *Granta* 48 (December 22, 2008).

AN AFRICAN ROADMAP

Everywhere,
the black tar wide and long
reaching even the land's horn
is divided by very thinly spread
white stains which run along its core
determining who goes in which
direction and who stops where.

The tar enraged,
chews itself from the edges.
It may consume itself completely
before it's free of the stain.

A REMARKABLE DAY IN THE CITY

Water flowed freely in my town today.
The municipality must have tapped into the Zambezi.

Officers made long standing rumours of water
shortages sound foolish as they carelessly
hosed down protestors in the town square.

Water poured over stunned bodies into blocked drains
washing away surface dirt along with any hopes
for a deep cleanse within city structures.
Water flowed freely in my town today.

The southern townships too had a distinct scent today.
Different to the usual smell of uncollected waste and
open sewers.

Officers introduced a new spicy aroma from tin
cans they threw in the streets to tone
down the stench of despair and civil disquiet.

The scent stung skin, eyes and nostrils.
I hear for two little ones it was the last fragrance
inhaled.
The southern township had a distinct scent today.

Water flowed freely in my town today
and everywhere was talk of a southern whiff.
But I don't recall anything from the leafy suburbs.
Nothing ever happens in northern suburbia.

FOOT IMPRESSIONS

When the snail's shell
crackles beneath the sole,
the ground a soft bump,
it's icky only momentarily,
a few taps of the heel
on the pavement,
the slimy mass slips off,
the memory is lost.

Is it the same for you
too, Mr. uniformed man,
when you crush the skulls
of kinsmen with your shiny boot?
Is the crackle the same,
the ickiness brief,
and is it just as easy
to shake off the memory?

WHAT NOT TO ASK

When the questions
were simple she quickly
obliged with excitement even,
sometimes with unsolicited
detail.

Other times dialogue ensued:
she would plump me on her lap,
 "do you understand sweetie?"
eyes teeming with
patience.

Other times, when questions
were more involved,
answers, if they came at all,
were curt and final:
"go play in the yard sweetie."

Soon I learned what to ask
and what not to ask.

Even now the rule holds.
When the questions are
simple, the answers are lengthy
chronicles heralded on the
morning and evening news.

When the questions come
more complex and inconvenient,

responses are blunt and grievous,
some we knew were buried
deep in the yard.

I think they want us
to learn what to ask
and what not to ask.

BLACK GOWN DZIDZAI*

We prepared!
Unlike the mystical African slackers who waste daylight
sharing folk tales out in the sun wrestling lizards for good spots,
we prepared!

Each day we arrived earlier than dawn, high on ambition,
thirsty for tricks to get ahead, futures so bright it was dizzying,
we prepared!

We learned the lines, bought the gowns, we readied for action
already calculating returns on sure investments as we were told,
God knows we prepared!

But here we are,
minds overdressed in devalued designs which cost our parents' pensions.
Here we are actors without a stage, wage or audience.

"Set yourself a stage on 5th,"
the old man says, blazer heavy on hunching shoulders.
Entrepreneurship the catchphrase of the season.
But this wasn't in the curriculum though!?!

Baffled, we stand by the way scratching heads for schemes
under and over qualified for this new stage direction   .
But how can this be?
We prepared!

Dzidzai: Shona name meaning Learn

NGWENYA*

That old crocodile gobbled down our neighbors
by the thousands last hurricane season,
but the village elders forbid the young men to hunt
and throw it in hell where such evils belong.
They say its tail can be salvaged
and will feed the nation.

Ngwenya: Shona word meaning crocodile

RAKING LEAVES

Today we'll rake again,
all of us around the base
of a tree which bears fruit
only on its highest branch.

We'll scrape beneath
a scorching sun which
penetrates barren branches
and seared scalps.

A people which suffers
no other seasons but the fall
for the leaves fall, and they fall
and they'll fall.

There will be no pips
between our teeth at day's end,
just dried leaves, so we'll build
all manner of castles with peat.

It's no wonder we mourn
excessively when we bury.
Just then we question the blisters
and arched backs,

and we recall the mocking bird
daily singing as if to taunt wasted efforts,
toil which occupies our everyday
yet affords no gain for the next.

But soon we jilt wit for belly,
each to his tool with tot and tune
to fill hollow dream chambers once
home to youthful desires.

We rake, amassing dried leaves.
No sooner are they gathered than they
are blown away by the slightest wind.
So we'll rake in perpetuity

until the rake depletes our strength
and the spade burrows a mouth
in the earth for the tree to devour
our shrivelled remains.

And those who remain will mourn
excessively as we're laid.
Just then they too will question
the blisters and arched backs
till dusk, when tomorrow beckons today.

And today, today we'll rake again.

WORSE THAN WOLVES

Daddy said to be on guard
against wolves in sheep's skin;
handsome types whose sweet
smiles conceal canines and
iron alloyed hearts.

But he spoke nothing
of hyenas in packs,
of the sickly ones whose
only strength is in numbers,
those who justify perversions

with vague mutterings
of feminine impropriety
and of a culture largely
unraveled and ignored save
for the few strands

which tangle women's
feet and throats so they never
wander and are never heard.

He made no mention
of these quasi-men who bear
no resemblance to our fathers
and forefathers, demigods
who cradled us in calloused hands.

Theirs is a different breed;
a mutation with unchecked
tongues, wayward fingers
and unmastered man parts.

Poor Eve, ill-equipped
to fight with nowhere to flee,
everywhere your groans
are muffled by an ensemble of
entitled baritones and basses.

Rich, poor, strong, weak alike
all unified in preserving a throne
on your back

THE "GODS" PREROGATIVE

When the gods wounded her
they meant for her to die.

She was not to scratch or salve.
She obeyed to her shallow grave.

He joined the clinic queue today.
The gods have repented.

THE RIPPERS

Her mother taught her to weave.
"Pull and fasten the strands tight,
two over, one under, again and again
till your unit is robust."

She herself proceeded
to hem down the edges.
There would be no extensions.

We, daughters of different totems,
must now rip the garment
from different angles,

so in mending
we may be stitched in.

FILED FOR SAFEKEEPING

I hide you in the deepest chamber
of my mind, only known to my
subconscious at specific hours
of the night when curious rays
won't force glimpses into truths
and untruth self-mastery cannot
yet grasp and there's a sparkle
in my eye so long as shadows hide
what I would rather not spy.

I met one with windows all
around his soul: brilliant gaping
openings at any one point
absorbing or reflecting light.
There's no hint of shadow
in him. I wonder how he
conceals his darker shades.

He loves to kiss my soul
deeply as though he attempts
to suck or blow at something
lodged at my core.
I know it's you he looks for
but I won't show him the trail.
He, too, will soon be exasperated
like the shrink who no longer
questions but faithfully
completes my prescriptions.

Some things simply cannot be shared
like dental floss or ear buds,
things that reach deep intimate places
jammed with filth foul even to the owner.
It's safer for all not to bring anyone there,
to the crypt beneath the soul
where ghosts of odious evils suffered
or embraced, lie undisturbed.

HOMESTRETCH

The last twenty minutes were most tiring.
I imagined Violet lying on their suede futon
feet crossed in the air, two pages away from completing
the reading assignment and proceeding to watch TV.

I imagined Rose who'd just now arrived home,
yanking shoes and socks off along the long corridor to her
bedroom before gulping a healthy dose of some sugary drink.
Just then, my journey became insufferable.

I would sit on the lower branches of the same rubber
tree around the corner from Rose's, de-scabbing
whatever graze I could find on my legs and arms.
In that time, I mastered the art of tenderly circling troubled areas,

uncovering parts now less sensitive,
affording the yet raw areas more time to heal,
and then sometimes, the last bit of scab on what had been
the most painful, tear- inducing spot, dropped off all on its own.

When I eventually got down from my tree,
home seemed within reach, the journey broken,
and what had been injured, restored by cover and time. Soon I, too,
would be chucking my sunrise reader, lips green from my sugary drink.

The end of the road appears very far today.
Some of those I walked with seem to have arrived already.
I imagine Violet finishing up the last few chapters of her doctorate
and Rose decorating her fourth baby's cake with some sugary frosting.

I imagine I need to find somewhere shady to be still for a time.

EVERYTHING BUT DIRT

The lenses are tainted
ash gray/brown from
decades of mass moral pollution.
All is murky, nothing is distinct.

Dirt is everything but dirt,
it's art, it's misunderstood,
it's rocks in transition,
but it's certainly not dirty.

Perhaps if dirt were simply dirt
the need to cleanse would be more apparent.

CLOUDS ARE GATHERING

Clouds are gathering overhead.
The wind's singing crescendos.
Everyone's shutting their windows
and swallows are waltzing the skies.

All are bracing for the storm.
I, too, should be running for cover,
but here I am lying face up
in an open meadow, thirsty.

I welcome the tempest's baptism,
exorcist of stubborn fears.
Countless trying droplets
push against the mind's

margins, deliberate breakers
determined to devastate and
reinstate in the same wash, a pond
plied into a pulsing river.

Surprising how strength becomes me.

ACKNOWLEDGMENTS

With grateful acknowledgment of the journals, reviews, and online publications which have provided a platform for me to publish some of the poems included in this collection. These include:

New Contrast Journal (South Africa), "Homestrech"
The Kalahari Review (Botswana), "Filed for Safekeeping"
The Badilisha Poetry Exchange, "Raking Leaves"